This book presented to:

Jackson

By:

Grand mom & Pépé

On:

Easter 2016

Best-Loved Easter Stories

CONCORDIA PUBLISHING HOUSE · SAINT LOUIS

Arch® Books

Published 2014 by Concordia Publishing House
3558 S. Jefferson Ave., St. Louis, MO 63118-3968
1-800-325-3040 • www.cph.org

Jesus Enters Jerusalem © 1993, 2004 Concordia
Publishing House

The Week that Led to Easter © 2001 Concordia
Publishing House

Good Friday © 1992 Concordia Publishing House

Barabbas Goes Free © 2003 Concordia Publishing House

The Resurrection © 2010 Concordia Publishing House

My Happy Easter Arch Book © 1996, 2003 Concordia
Publishing House

Manufactured in Shenzhen, China/55760/300510

1 2 3 4 5 6 7 8 9 10   23 22 21 20 19 18 17 16 15 14

Table of Contents

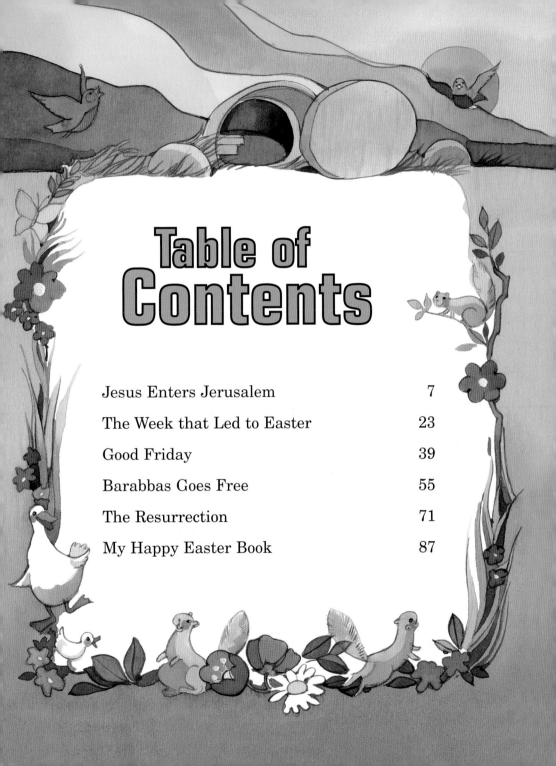

Jesus Enters Jerusalem   7

The Week that Led to Easter   23

Good Friday   39

Barabbas Goes Free   55

The Resurrection   71

My Happy Easter Book   87

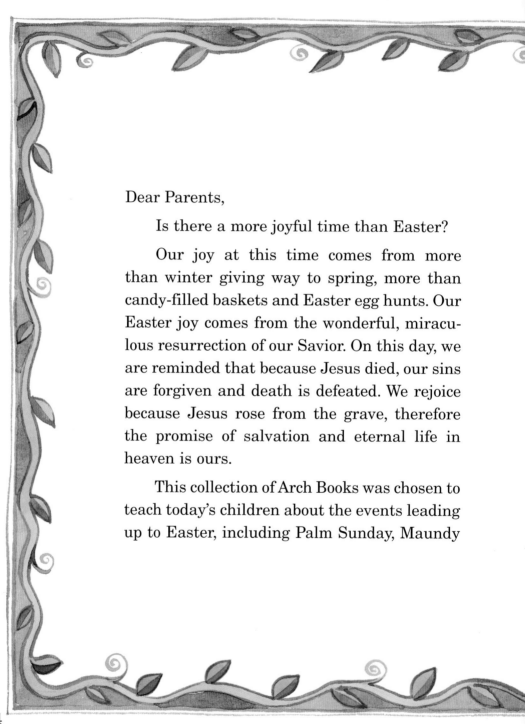

Dear Parents,

Is there a more joyful time than Easter?

Our joy at this time comes from more than winter giving way to spring, more than candy-filled baskets and Easter egg hunts. Our Easter joy comes from the wonderful, miraculous resurrection of our Savior. On this day, we are reminded that because Jesus died, our sins are forgiven and death is defeated. We rejoice because Jesus rose from the grave, therefore the promise of salvation and eternal life in heaven is ours.

This collection of Arch Books was chosen to teach today's children about the events leading up to Easter, including Palm Sunday, Maundy

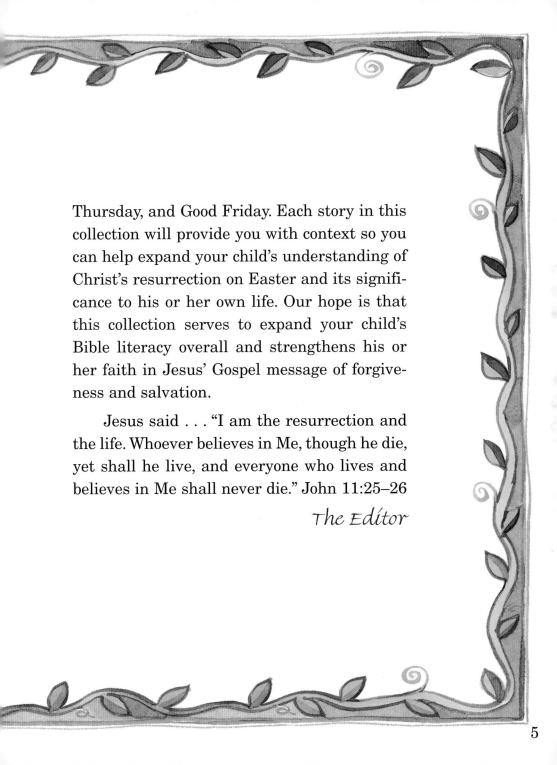

Thursday, and Good Friday. Each story in this collection will provide you with context so you can help expand your child's understanding of Christ's resurrection on Easter and its significance to his or her own life. Our hope is that this collection serves to expand your child's Bible literacy overall and strengthens his or her faith in Jesus' Gospel message of forgiveness and salvation.

Jesus said . . . "I am the resurrection and the life. Whoever believes in Me, though he die, yet shall he live, and everyone who lives and believes in Me shall never die." John 11:25–26

The Editor

Jesus Enters Jerusalem

Matthew 21:1–11, Mark 11:1–11,
Luke 19:28–38, John 12:12–19
for children

Written by Jane L. Fryar
Illustrated by Michelle Dorenkamp

In spring of each and every year,
God's people came from far and near
To tell what their great God had done,
To shout the victory He had won.

"Let's praise our Lord who set us free
From Pharaoh and from slavery."
"You've saved us, God!" the people sang.
Along the road their glad song rang.

As Jesus neared the city gate,
He paused and asked His friends to wait.
He looked at them, then said to two,
"I have a job for you … and you."

"Go to the village over there.
Look for two donkeys—colt and mare.
Untie them. Bring them here to Me.
I need them, as you soon will see.

"If someone tries to stop you, say,
'The Master sent us here today.
He needs the colt. Please, let us do
What our Lord Jesus told us to.'"

11

So off the two disciples sped,
Found everything as Jesus said,
Untied the donkeys, walked away.
And then a voice rang out: "Wait! Hey!"

But Jesus' friends knew what to say:
"The Master sent us here today.
He needs the colt. Please let us do
What our Lord Jesus told us to."

The donkey's owner nodded. Then,
He sent the colt with Jesus' men.
They hurried back up toward the road
To find the Lord, as they'd been told.

The little donkey walked along
Into the city while the song
That told of God's great love rang out,
And Jesus heard the people shout.

"Hosanna, Jesus! You're our King!
Hosanna! Save! To You we sing!
Hosanna! Praise! We shout again.
Hosanna! Praise! Amen! Amen!"

16

Then someone cut a palm branch flag.
And someone else began to drag
His outer cloak upon the street,
Right under Jesus' donkey's feet.

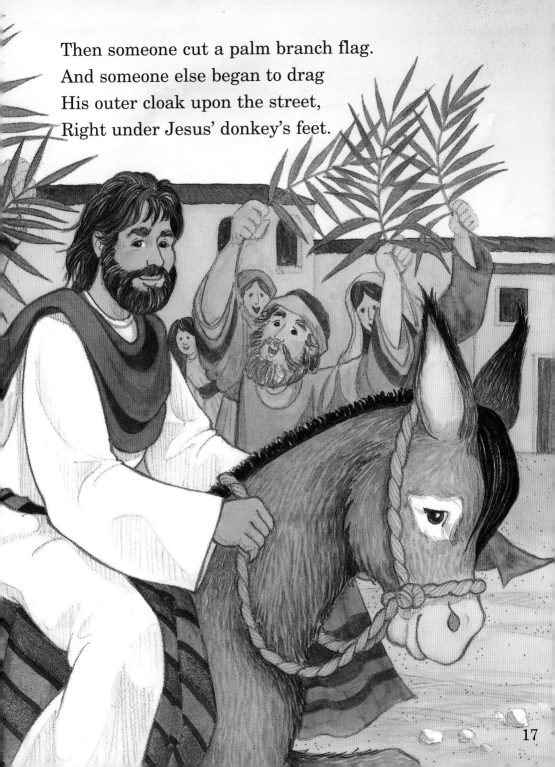

The Savior knew that this glad song
Would turn to hate before too long.
He knew what He in love would do
To save all people—me and you.

He saw the cross. He knew that there
Our loneliness and pain He'd bear.
Still on He rode to death and grave
And resurrection. On to save!

"You've saved us, Lord! Today we sing!
Hosanna! You're the Lord, our King!
Hosanna! Praise! We shout again.
Hosanna! Praise! Amen! Amen!"

Dear Parents:

The crowds that came to Jerusalem to celebrate the Passover during the third year of Jesus' earthly ministry cheered Him as their king, their deliverer.

"Hosanna! Save us, Lord!" they shouted.

Five short days later, a mob, perhaps made up of many of the same people, roared, "Away with this man! Crucify Him!"

The crowd didn't understand Jesus. They didn't want the kind of king God the Father had planned for them. They wanted freedom from Roman rule. Jesus came to free them from Satan's power. They wanted deliverance from Roman occupation and taxation. Jesus came to deliver them from sin and the fear of death.

Although many people today still reject Jesus and His kingdom, He continues to offer us life in that kingdom, as well as forgiveness, freedom, joy, and peace. As you read and talk with your child about the day we call Palm Sunday, celebrate the new life Jesus has given you.

The Editor

THE WEEK THAT LED TO EASTER

The Story of Holy Week Matthew 21:1–28:10; Mark 11:1–16:8;
Luke 19:29–24:12; and John 12:12–20:10 for children

Written by Joanne Larrison
Illustrated by Jenny Williams

"Hosanna! Sing to Christ the King,"
Crowds shouted as He came.
They had heard the many stories—
How He healed the sick and lame.

Jerusalem was crowded.
The Passover had begun—
A time to remember Egypt,
And to have a little fun.

The 12 disciples led the way
To the upper room
Where Jesus shared His final meal—
He knew His life was doomed.

He told them that His life would end,
And that He'd be betrayed.
He shared His bread and wine with them,
Then bowed His head and prayed.

27

Jesus asked to be remembered
For the sins He'd take away.
He told them of God's final plan
And that He could not stay.

Then He prayed to God to guide Him—
To give strength along the way.
For He understood the suff'ring
And the price that He must pay.

29

The leaders and guards were waiting
To take Him away from town.
They would nail Him to a wooden cross,
Place on His head a thorny crown.

They had turned the crowd against Him,
Said, "He's *not* God's Son to fear."
And the crowd yelled, "CRUCIFY Him!"
Jesus did not shed a tear.

The sky turned black and thunder rolled.
Jesus said His final words:
"Please forgive them, Father."
"It is finished!" they then heard.

Friends sealed Him in a cold, dark cave
With a big stone for a door.
Not many came to see Him,
For the crowds—they cared no more.

Though God's plan now seemed completed
To the people here on earth,
Christ's death was just the beginning—
A new chance for our rebirth.

For when Jesus died, He died to save
All people great and small.
He took our sins away from us—
'Twas the greatest gift of all.

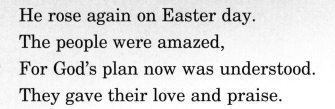

He rose again on Easter day.
The people were amazed,
For God's plan now was understood.
They gave their love and praise.

Jesus is *still* alive today.
He reigns in heaven above.
He forgives us and He guides us,
And fills our hearts with love.

Dear Parents:

The week that led to Easter is significant in the lives of Christians. It is a sober time, tracing the steps of Christ to the cross. Yet it leads to jubilant celebration as Christ defeats Satan and sin, opening the door of heaven to all believers.

The week that led to Easter is called "Holy Week," and it is indeed holy. It frames the New Testament fulfillment of God's Old Testament promise to send a Savior. It is a week worth commemorating.

Set aside time as a family to review what happened during Holy Week. Check out the Bible references on page 23, and decide which to use. Read a portion of the Passion story each day from Palm Sunday to Easter. After each reading, ask your children to retell that portion of the story using their own words. Raid your closets for suitable props and costumes. Act out the story, trying to include all the characters— even the crowd that yells, "Crucify Him!" In so doing, the week that led to Easter will take on new meaning and be holy indeed.

The Editor

GOOD FRIDAY

Matthew 21:1–27:61
Mark 11:1–15:47
Luke 19:28–23:56
John 12:12–19:42
for children

Written by Louise Ulmer
Illustrated by Reg Sandland

Why do we say, "*Good* Friday"
When we speak of the day Jesus died?
Wasn't it a most terrible day,
A day all believers cried?

Although it seemed like a hopeless day
When Jesus laid down His life,
It was part of the plan God had for His world
To make all the wrong things right.

The story on Palm Sunday,
When Jesus rode into town.
"Hosanna to the king!" shouted followers,
As they spread green palm leaves down.

But Jesus had powerful enemies,
And His words often made them mad.
They decided to get even.
By saying Jesus was bad.

Thursday, in the cool of the night,
When most of His friends were at home,
Jesus took His disciples to a garden.
They slept while He prayed alone.

Men marched to the garden with clubs and swords
While He told His disciples to pray.
When the crowd took Him to the high priest,
His disciples ran away.

The high priest sent Jesus to Pilate
On Friday, before the first light.
God would give the life of His Son
To make all the wrong things right.

Angry men made fun of Jesus.
Someone made Him a thorny crown.
His enemies gave Him a purple robe.
Others hit Him and pushed Him down.

"Behold your king," Governor Pilate cried.
"I'll punish Him and send Him home."
"We have no king but Caesar," the chief priests lied,
For those men had hearts of stone.

"Kill Him! Crucify Jesus!"
Shouted voices hateful and loud.
Pilate washed his hands of the problem
And gave in to the angry crowd.

Soldiers nailed Him to a cross,
   Then planted it in the ground.
   "Save Yourself!" laughed His enemies.
But Jesus made not a sound.

As Jesus hung upon the cross
He knew His work was almost through.
He prayed to His heavenly Father,
"Forgive them; they know not what they do."

The Son of God was dying.
Darkness covered the sun.
Jesus gave up His spirit and breathed His last;
His work on earth was done.

But though Jesus died and was buried,
The world had a great surprise.
For in three days, just as He promised,
Jesus would awaken and rise.

So you see, it was a glad day
When Jesus laid down His life.
'Cause God raised Him to life again
To make all our wrong things right.

Dear Parents:

It is natural for your child to wonder why we call the day Jesus died "good." Your child may also wonder why anyone would want to kill Jesus—our best Friend and Savior. Explain to your child that we deserve to be punished for our sins, the bad things we do. But because God loves us so much, He sent His only Son to die in our place (John 3:16). God worked through the events of history, including the jealousy and fear of some religious leaders, to carry out His plan.

God's good plan rescued us from eternal death in hell. As Jesus died, He cried, "It is finished" (John 19:30). His redeeming work on earth was completed and He died as a victor.

Help your child understand the "good" in Good Friday—the goodness of a loving God who gives His children the gift of eternal life through the death and resurrection of His Son.

The Editor

54

Barabbas Goes Free

The Story of the Release of Barabbas

Matthew 27:15–26, Mark 15:6–15, Luke 23:13–25,
and John 18:39–40 for children

Erik J. Rottmann
Illustrated by JoAnn E. Kitchel

55

At Passover in Israel,
The greatest and the least
All gathered in Jerusalem
To celebrate the feast.

Now Pontius Pilate had a way
To make the people glad.
At Passover he would set free
A prisoner he had.

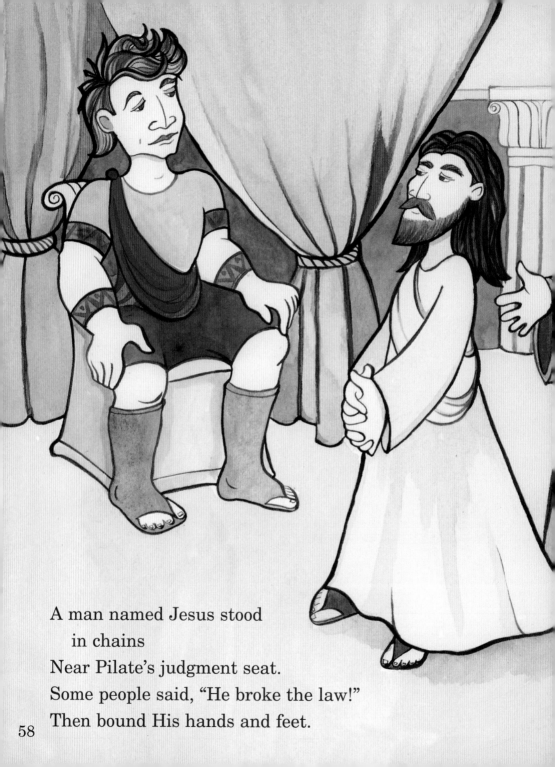

A man named Jesus stood
   in chains
Near Pilate's judgment seat.
Some people said, "He broke the law!"
Then bound His hands and feet.

The soldiers had another man
Imprisoned in a cell.
Barabbas broke so many laws
The people knew him well.

God tells us with the
    fourth command,
"Obey the government."
Barabbas would not listen to
The leaders God had sent.

God also says, "You shall not kill."
Barabbas did not mind.
He drew his sword and took a life.
He acted so unkind!

Barabbas also stole some things,
In a vicious way.
The punishment for all his crimes
Was now his debt to pay.

But Jesus had done nothing wrong.
He had no debt to pay.
So Pilate said, "I'll set Him free!"
The people yelled, "No WAY!"

"We want Barabbas!" they all cried,
"Barabbas is our guy!"
"But what of Jesus?" Pilate asked.
"He shouldn't have to die!"

The people just grew angrier.
"We ALL want Jesus dead!
And if His death makes you feel bad,
We'll take the blame instead!"

Pontius Pilate feared the crowd.
He wanted to keep peace.
He washed his hands, and then he gave
Barabbas his release.

So there stood Jesus, innocent.
He never broke a rule.
He traded places with the man
Who always had been cruel.

The soldiers came and took our Lord
And whipped Him for their boss.
They put some thorns upon His head,
Then made Him drag His cross.

The Bible says that you and I
Both owed a debt of sin,
Because of all we say and do,
And evil thoughts within.

But Jesus Christ gave up His life
In death upon a tree.
Just as He took Barabbas's place—
Christ also set US free.

You, like Barabbas, have God's gift
Of freedom from your sin.
And Jesus rose, so now you'll live
Eternally with Him!

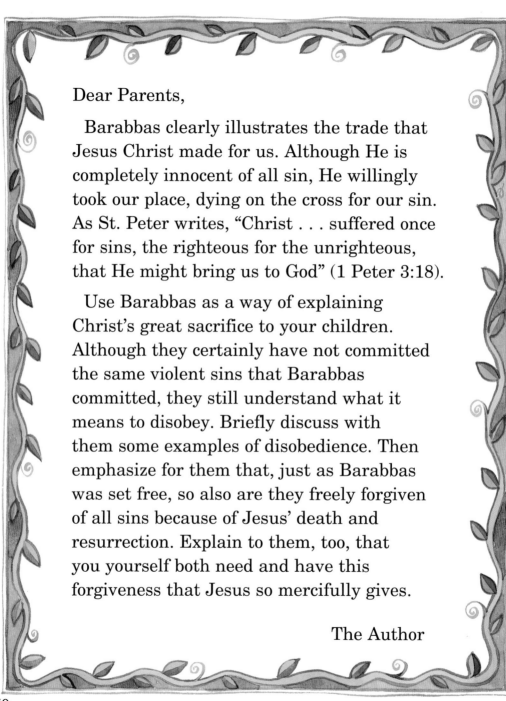

Dear Parents,

Barabbas clearly illustrates the trade that Jesus Christ made for us. Although He is completely innocent of all sin, He willingly took our place, dying on the cross for our sin. As St. Peter writes, "Christ . . . suffered once for sins, the righteous for the unrighteous, that He might bring us to God" (1 Peter 3:18).

Use Barabbas as a way of explaining Christ's great sacrifice to your children. Although they certainly have not committed the same violent sins that Barabbas committed, they still understand what it means to disobey. Briefly discuss with them some examples of disobedience. Then emphasize for them that, just as Barabbas was set free, so also are they freely forgiven of all sins because of Jesus' death and resurrection. Explain to them, too, that you yourself both need and have this forgiveness that Jesus so mercifully gives.

The Author

THE Resurrection

Isaiah 53:4–6 and Matthew 21:1–11; 26;
27:27–66; 28:1–10 for Children

Written by Cynda Strong
Illustrated by Helen Cann

Isaiah's message had foretold
How Christ would save all men:
He'd take upon Himself our sins;
He'd die and rise again.

And so His time on earth did pass,
And many friends did gain,
For He became their earthly lord;
They thought on earth He'd reign.

With palms and garments spread before,
Without a crown of gold,
Our Lord went to Jerusalem
And on a donkey rode.

In parables He taught them all
To live their lives on earth,
To know salvation's gift from God,
The gift of greatest worth.

And Judas, one of Jesus' friends,
Told priests what Jesus claimed.
Denying Him for payment gold,
"Betrayer" he was named.

And so the Twelve made plans to meet,
The Passover was near.
A final meal with Christ they'd eat;
His lessons they would hear.

And at this final meal, our Lord
Served them the wine and bread.
"This is My body and My blood,"
To them our Savior said.

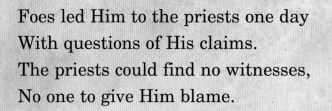

Foes led Him to the priests one day
With questions of His claims.
The priests could find no witnesses,
No one to give Him blame.

To Pilate's seat they took our Lord.
Though Pilate found no wrong,
He sentenced Him to die that day,
His suff'ring would be long.

Upon His head they placed a crown
Of thorns to mock His name.
They spat and yelled and struck His head,
Denouncing Jesus' claim.

They placed Him high upon a cross
And pierced His side with spear.
They placed a sign above His head,
And loudly they did jeer.

The sky turned dark when Jesus died;
He suffered with great pain.
He bore the sins of all that day,
Our home in heav'n to gain.

Then three days passed and Sunday came;
His friends went to His tomb.
But when the women went inside,
They saw that He was gone.

The angels sang with joy that day;
No longer was Christ dead.
He'd conquered sin and death for us,
Just as God's Word had said!

Then joyful praise to God in heav'n,
Like angels we can sing.
For Christ has risen from the dead,
Our Savior and our King!

Dear Parents,

Centuries before the birth of Christ, the prophet Isaiah told not only of His birth but also of His death. With Christ's birth, the fulfillment of the prophecy of God's plan for our salvation began.

Christ grew into manhood, preached, and taught among the people. They watched Him perform miracles, heal the sick, and give hope to the oppressed.

At the end of His three-year ministry, Christ began His journey that would end with His death on the cross. He rode into Jerusalem on the back of a young donkey on the day we celebrate as Palm Sunday—not exactly the triumphant royal entry the people had expected. But Jesus was not meant to be a king on earth.

During those next days, He dined with His faithful followers and encouraged them to keep their faith. He presented the meal we call the Lord's Supper. He was betrayed by one of His faithful and suffered the emotional anguish of being abandoned by God.

As you read the Easter story to your child, he will see the reason we can sing "Alleluia" with the angels. The stone was rolled away. The tomb was empty. Jesus has risen. Now we are assured of our salvation.

Alleluia! He lives!

The Author

My Happy Easter Book

Matthew 27:57–28:10 for Children

Written by Gloria A. Truitt
Illustrated by Len Ebert

When Jesus died upon the cross,
    His friends looked on and cried;
For they had lost their Master,
    Their Lord and loving Guide.

89

A friend wrapped Jesus' body in
Fine linens; then he laid
Our Lord within his family tomb—
A cave that he had made.

To make sure no one could go in,
He rolled a giant stone
Across the entrance; closing it.
Now Jesus was alone.

91

While Jesus suffered on the cross,
    Two women watched nearby.
They both were grieving for their Lord,
    And, oh, how they did cry.

Both women were called Mary, and
    They loved the Lord, you see.
And, two days later they were filled
    With curiosity.

To the tomb they ran with speed.
They had to take a look!
All at once an earthquake struck . . .
Imagine how they shook!

An angel told them Christ was gone,
"He's risen from the dead!
Now, quickly go to Galilee
And spread the news!" he said.

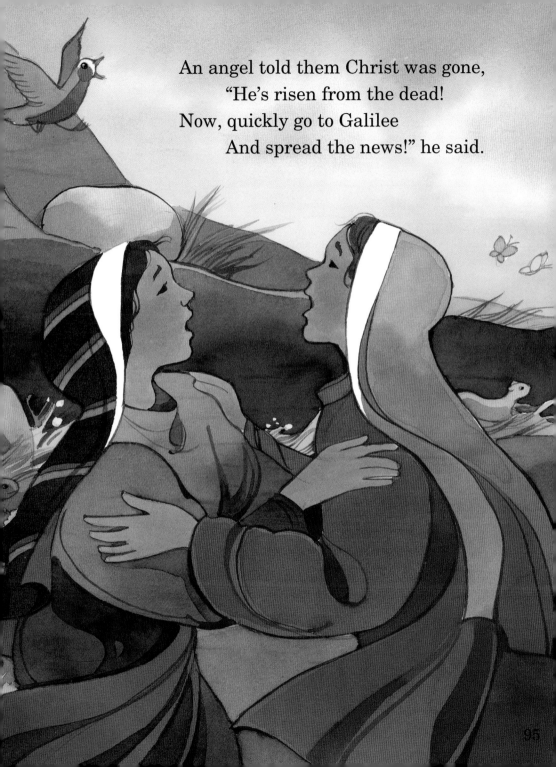

So the women hurried off—
  Their hearts were filled with gladness.
"It must be true! He lives again!"
  No longer they felt sadness.

Then suddenly the women met
Christ Jesus on the way!
"Yes, it's Me!" the Savior said
On that first Easter day.

The happy time of Easter comes
    Every year in spring
When, following the winter's chill,
    We hear the robins sing.

Now everywhere we look it seems
    That fresh, new life is seen—
From budding trees to crawly worms,
    And many sprouts of green.

Praise God, for it is wonderful
That Jesus came to earth.
He died, but rose to live again,
So *we* could have new birth!

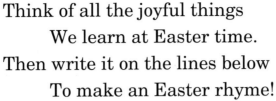

Think of all the joyful things
We learn at Easter time.
Then write it on the lines below
To make an Easter rhyme!

My Easter Poem

_____

_____

_____

_____

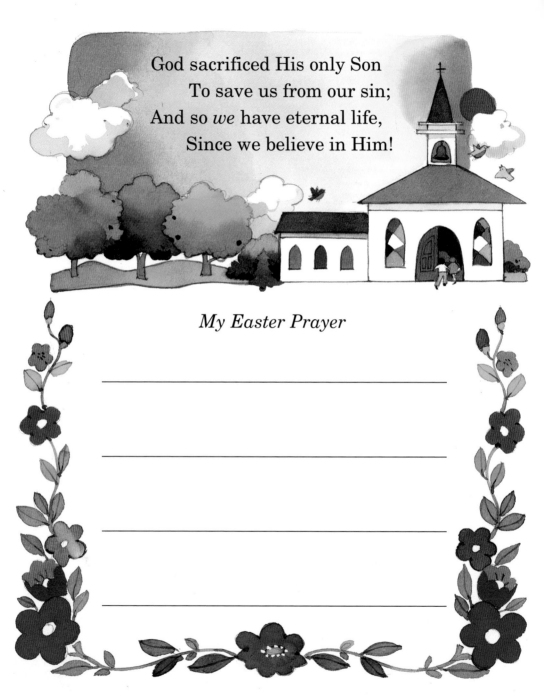

God sacrificed His only Son
To save us from our sin;
And so *we* have eternal life,
Since we believe in Him!

My Easter Prayer

_____

_____

_____

_____

The Arch® Book Bible Story Library

Bible Beginnings

59-1577	The Fall into Sin
59-1534	The First Brothers
59-2206	A Man Named Noah
59-1511	Noah's 2-by-2 Adventure
59-1560	The Story of Creation
59-2239	Where Did the World Come From?

The Old Testament

59-1502	Abraham's Big Test
59-2244	Abraham, Sarah, and Isaac
59-2229	Daniel and the Lions
59-1559	David and Goliath
59-1593	David and His Friend Jonathan
59-2220	Deborah Saves the Day
59-1543	Elijah Helps the Widow
59-2251	Ezekiel and the Dry Bones
59-1567	The Fiery Furnace
59-1570	God Calls Abraham . . . God Calls You!
59-1587	God Provides Victory through Gideon
59-1523	God's Fire for Elijah
59-1542	Good News for Naaman
59-2223	How Enemies Became Friends
59-2247	Isaac Blesses Jacob and Esau
59-1538	Jacob's Dream
59-1539	Jericho's Tumbling Walls
59-2246	Jonah, the Runaway Prophet
59-1514	Jonah and the Very Big Fish
59-2233	Joseph, Jacob's Favorite Son
59-2216	King Josiah and God's Book
59-1583	The Lord Calls Samuel
59-2219	Moses and the Bronze Snake
59-1607	Moses and the Long Walk
59-2266	The Mystery of the Moving Hand
59-1535	A Mother Who Prayed
59-2249	One Boy, One Stone, One God
59-2253	Queen Esther Visits the King
59-2211	Ruth and Naomi
59-2276	Samson
59-1586	The Ten Commandments
59-1608	The Ten Plagues
59-2263	The Tower of Babel
59-1550	Tiny Baby Moses
59-1530	Tried and True Job
59-2260	The 23rd Psalm
59-1603	Zerubbabel Rebuilds the Temple

The New Testament

59-1580	The Coming of the Holy Spirit
59-2259	The Great Commission
59-2207	His Name Is John
59-1532	Jailhouse Rock
59-1520	Jesus and the Family Trip
59-2277	Jesus and the Rich Young Man
59-1588	Jesus Calls His Disciples
59-2215	Jesus Shows His Glory
59-2270	Lydia Believes
59-1521	Mary and Martha's Dinner Guest
59-2269	Nicodemus and Jesus
59-2227	Paul's Great Basket Caper
59-2267	The Pentecost Story
59-1578	Philip and the Ethiopian
59-1601	Saul's Conversion
59-1574	Timothy Joins Paul
59-2222	Twelve Ordinary Men
59-1599	Zacchaeus

Arch® Book Companions

59-2232	The Fruit of the Spirit
59-1609	God, I've Gotta Talk to You
59-1575	The Lord's Prayer
59-1562	My Happy Birthday Book
59-2271	Best-Loved Christmas Stories
59-2272	Best-Loved Parables of Jesus
59-2273	Best-Loved Miracles of Jesus
59-2274	Best-Loved Easter Stories

Christmas Arch® Books

59-1579	Baby Jesus Is Born
59-1544	Baby Jesus Visits the Temple
59-1553	Born on Christmas Morn
59-2261	The Christmas Angels
59-1605	The Christmas Message
59-2225	The Christmas Promise
59-1546	Joseph's Christmas Story
59-1499	Mary's Christmas Story
59-1584	My Merry Christmas Arch® Book
59-2252	Oh, Holy Night!
59-1537	On a Silent Night
59-2243	Once Upon a Clear Dark Night
59-2234	The Shepherds Shook in Their Shoes
59-2268	The Songs of Christmas
59-1594	Star of Wonder
59-2209	When Jesus Was Born

Easter Arch® Books

59-1551	Barabbas Goes Free
59-2205	The Centurion at the Cross
59-1516	The Day Jesus Died
59-2213	The Easter Gift
59-2221	The Easter Stranger
59-2275	The Easter Surprise
59-1602	The Easter Victory
59-2265	From Adam to Easter
59-1582	Good Friday
59-1585	Jesus Enters Jerusalem
59-1561	Jesus Returns to Heaven
59-2248	John's Easter Story
59-1592	Mary Magdalene's Easter Story
59-1564	My Happy Easter Arch® Book
59-2258	The Gardens of Easter
59-2231	The Resurrection
59-1517	The Story of the Empty Tomb
59-1504	Thomas, the Doubting Disciple
59-1501	The Very First Lord's Supper
59-1541	The Week That Led to Easter

Parables and Lessons of Jesus

59-2257	Jesus and the Canaanite Woman
59-1589	Jesus and the Woman at the Well
59-1500	Jesus Blesses the Children
59-1595	Jesus, My Good Shepherd
59-2245	Jesus Teaches Us Not to Worry
59-1540	Jesus Washes Peter's Feet
59-2264	The Lesson of the Tree and Its Fruit
59-1606	The Lost Coin
59-2235	The Parable of the Ten Bridesmaids
59-2218	The Parable of the Lost Sheep
59-2224	The Parable of the Prodigal Son
59-2262	The Parable of the Seeds
59-2210	The Parable of the Talents
59-2254	The Parable of the Woman and the Judge
59-2250	The Parable of the Workers in the Vineyard
59-1512	The Seeds That Grew and Grew
59-1503	The Story of Jesus' Baptism and Temptation
59-1596	The Story of the Good Samaritan
59-2214	The Widow's Offering
59-2208	The Wise and Foolish Builders

Miracles Jesus Performed

59-1531	Down through the Roof
59-1568	Get Up, Lazarus!
59-1604	The Great Catch of Fish
59-1581	Jesus Calms the Storm
59-1598	Jesus' First Miracle
59-2230	Jesus Heals Blind Bartimaeus
59-2255	Jesus Heals the Man at the Pool
59-2236	Jesus Heals the Centurion's Servant
59-2226	Jesus Wakes the Little Girl
59-1597	Jesus Walks on the Water
59-1558	A Meal for Many
59-2212	The Thankful Leper
59-1510	What's for Lunch